ANGELINE GORMLEY

SPEECH
DELAY
WORKBOOK

FOR KiDS

HELPS YOUR CHILD USE WORDS TO FORM PHRASES AND SENTENCES

Introduction

Welcome to Speech Delay Workbook for Kids. This speech delay book is intended to help your child's expressive language skills, primarily their ability to use words to form words, phrases, and sentences. When searching for speech delay books for toddlers, you'd find that many of them don't have a specific structure or instruction for parents and educators to use.

Since speech and developmental delays can vary for every child, this workbook tackles different areas of language syntax that can be used in daily conversation. It is ideal when looking for books for kids with speech delay or speech delay books for parents — every section has instructions to help adults facilitate the activity.

We hope that you found this speech delay workbook useful. If you found this resource valuable, please give us a 5-star rating on Amazon, as we donate a portion of our proceeds to St. Jude Children's Hospital and Tim Tebow Foundation, charities that help children with cancer and special needs. Thank you very much!

GREETINGS

When we want to greet someone, we say "Hi" and their name. These are all people with their names. Let's pretend to greet them.

First, I'll point to "Hi," and then I'll point to the person. I'll help you say "hi" to them, and then it will be your turn to do it on your own. (You can extend this to practicing greetings with people around you as well).

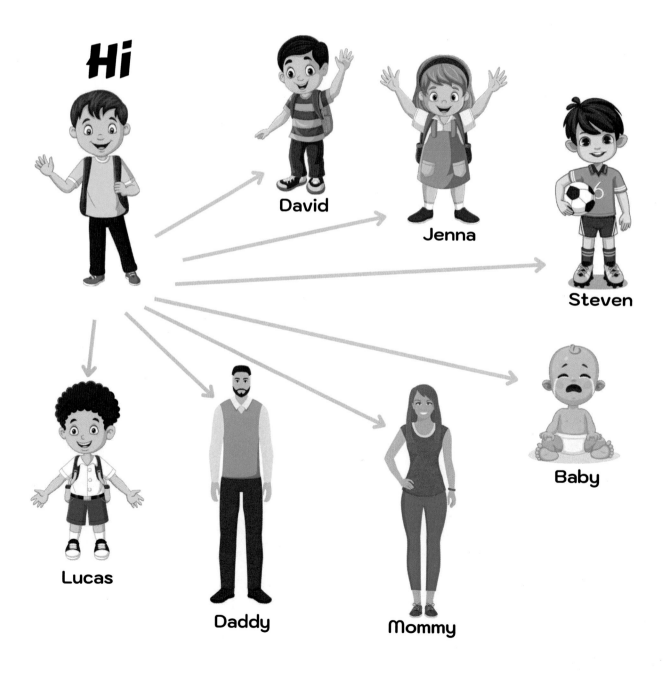

GREETINGS

Hi

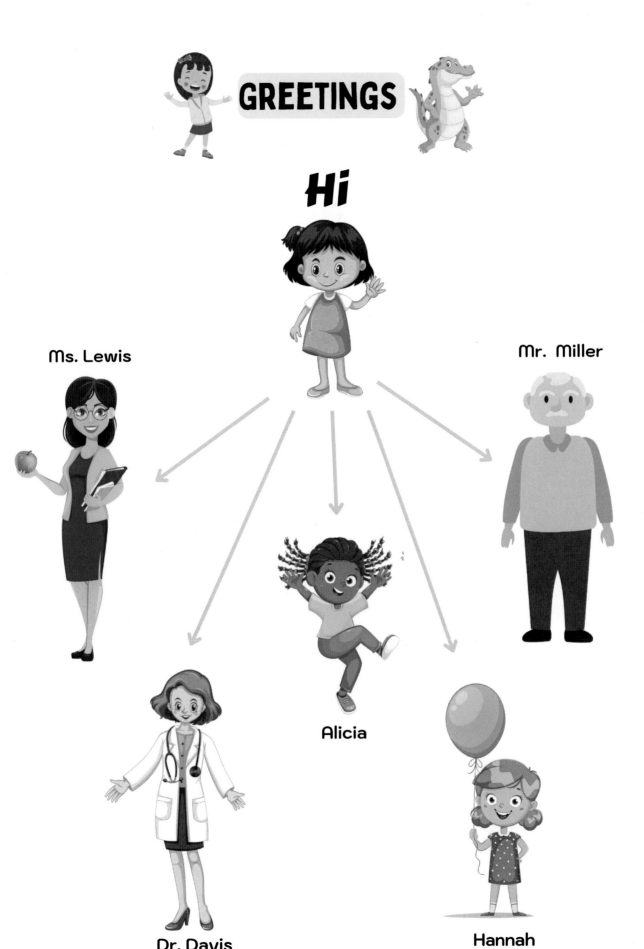

Ms. Lewis

Mr. Miller

Dr. Davis

Alicia

Hannah

PHRASES FOR ASSISTANCE

Sometimes you need assistance to do tasks. You can say "help" followed by the action you need assistance with, such as washing your hands, carrying an object, or using the restroom.

Let's practice the word "help." I will point to these images and together we will say it, then it will be your turn to speak it.

PHRASES FOR ASSISTANCE

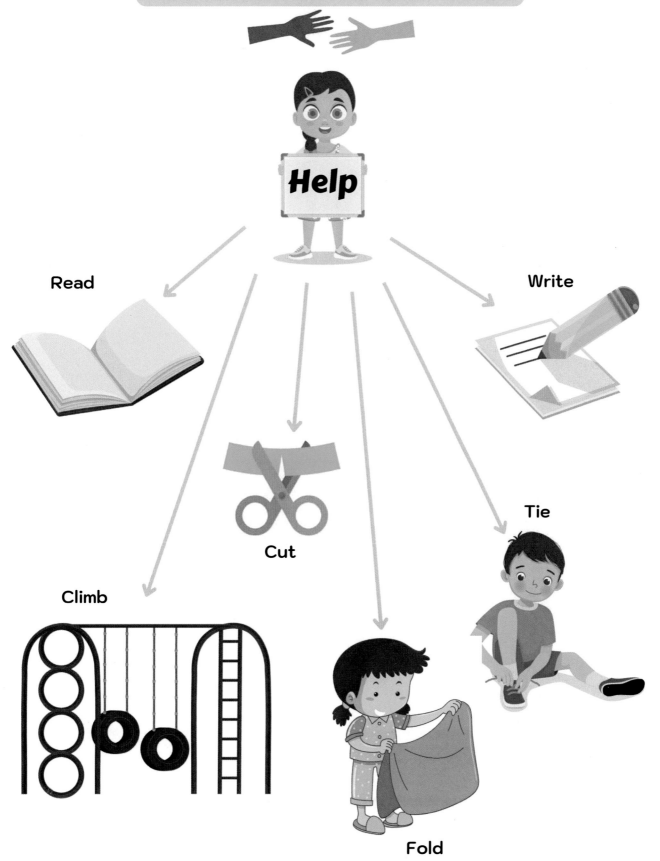

Help

Read

Write

Cut

Tie

Climb

Fold

FACILITATING VERB + OBJECT (FOOD)

There are different kinds of food. When we want to eat anything, we say "eat" followed by the food's name. I'll say "eat" and then point to the food. I will help you in saying it first, and then it'll be your turn to say both words on your own.

FACILITATING VERB + OBJECT (FOOD)

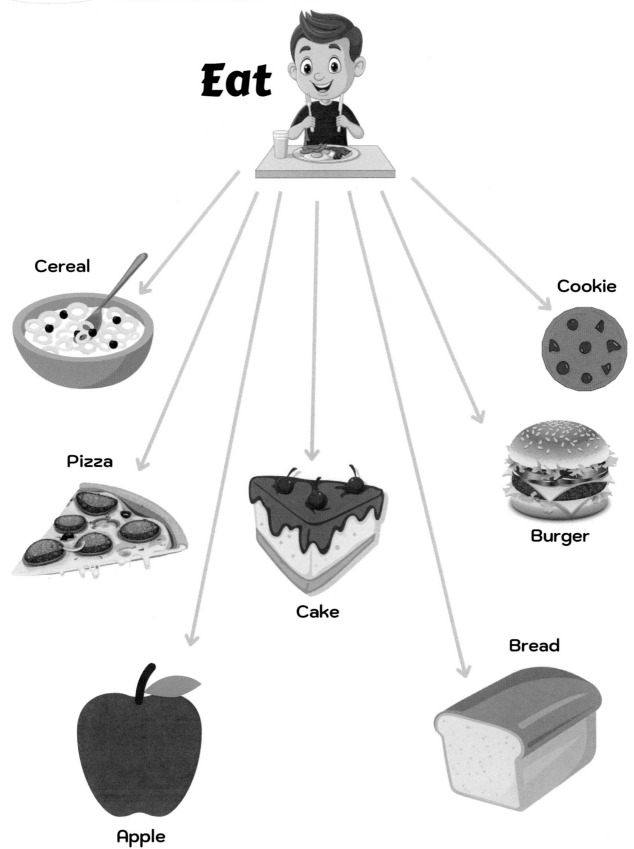

Eat

Cereal

Cookie

Pizza

Cake

Burger

Apple

Bread

FACILITATING VERB + OBJECT (TOYS)

There are different kinds of toys. When we want to play with a toy, we say "play" followed by the toy's name. I'll say "play" and then point to the toy. I will assist you in saying it first, and then it'll be your turn to say both words on your own.

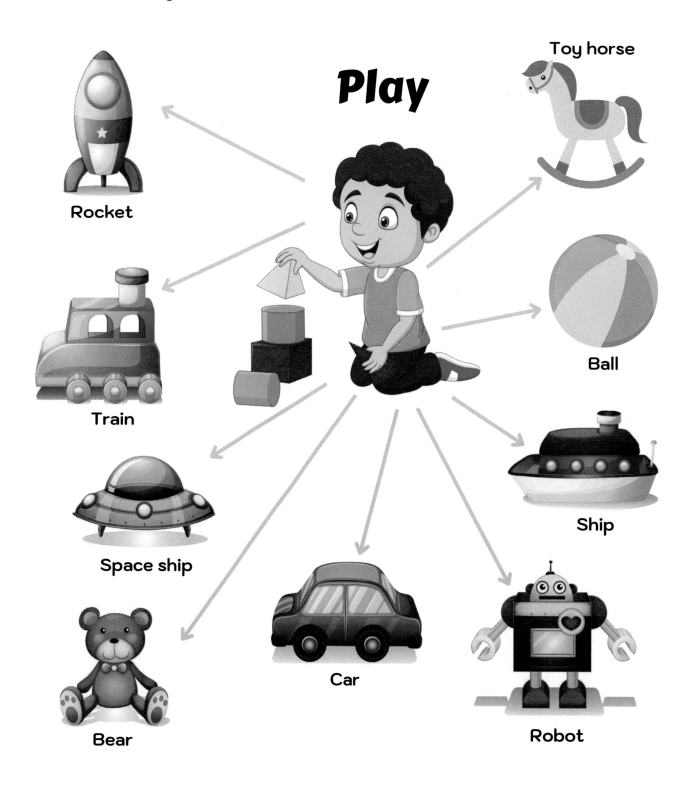

Toy horse

Play

Rocket

Train

Ball

Space ship

Ship

Bear

Car

Robot

FACILITATING VERB + OBJECT (TOYS)

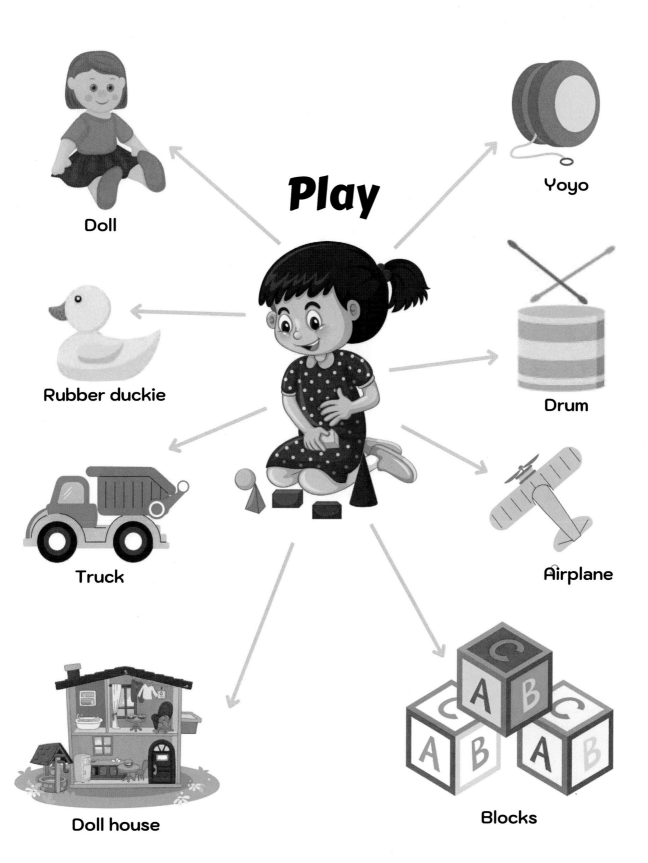

Doll

Yoyo

Play

Rubber duckie

Drum

Truck

Airplane

Doll house

Blocks

FACILITATING VERB + OBJECT (VEHICLES)

All of these are different kinds of vehicles. We say "ride" followed by the name of the vehicle we want to use. I'll point to the word "ride" and then to the vehicle. First, I'll help you say it, and then you can say both words on your own.

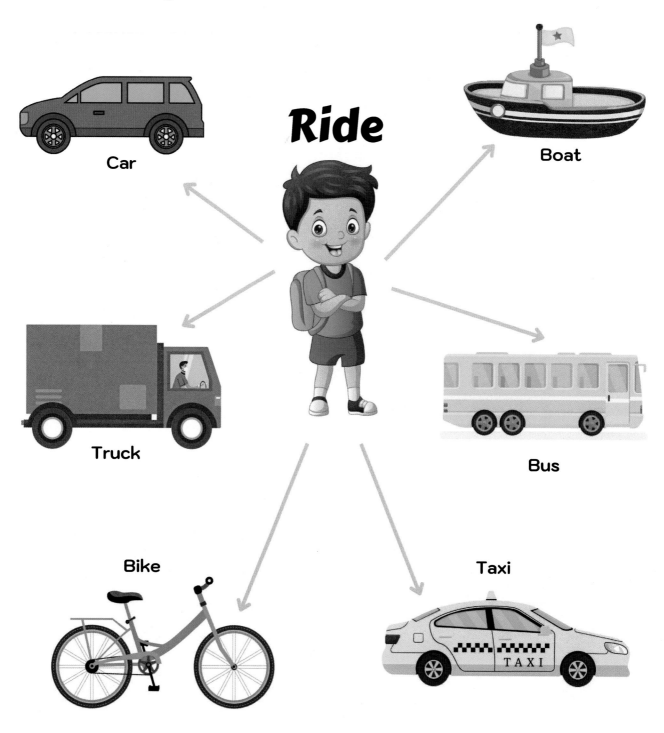

Car

Ride

Boat

Truck

Bus

Bike

Taxi

FACILITATING VERB + OBJECT (VEHICLES)

Ride

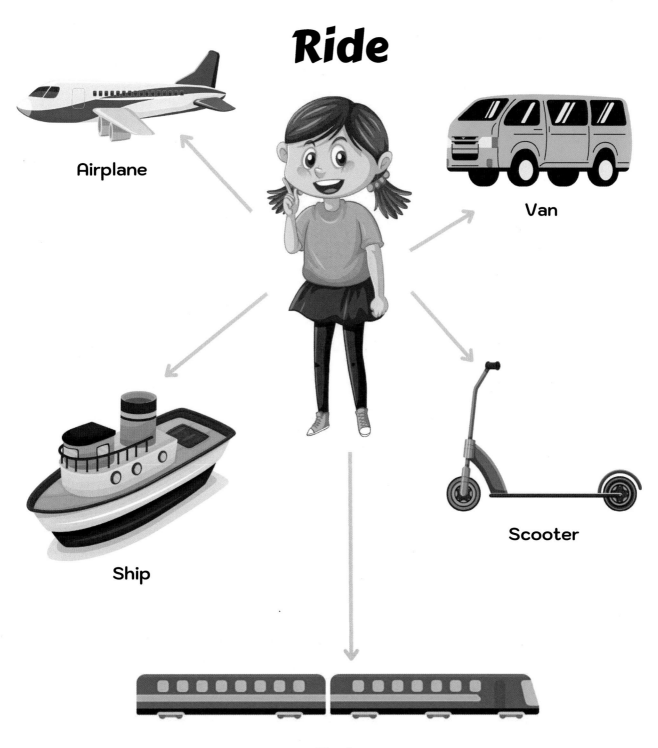

Airplane

Van

Ship

Scooter

Train

FACILITATING SUBJECT + VERB (SELF)

You do many different things. You do things at home, at school, and in other places. When you want to let someone know that you are doing something, you use "I" followed by the activity's name.

Let's draw or place a photo of you on the letter "I." We will say "I" followed by your activity. I'll point to it, and we'll say it together. Then it will be your turn to say it on your own.

FACILITATING SUBJECT + VERB (SELF)

I

Play

Watch

Dance

Catch

Bake

Sing

Slide

FACILITATING SUBJECT + VERB (OTHERS)

People do lots of different things. They do things at home, at school, and in other places. When you want to say that someone is doing something, you say their name first, followed by the activity's name.

Below are the names of three different people. We will say their names, followed by their actions. I will point to it, and we will say it together, then you will say it alone.

Eric   Olivia   James

Brushes

Eats

Drinks

Laughs

Cleans

Writes

FACILITATING SUBJECT + VERB (OTHERS)

Mr. Jones   **Mom**   **Dad**

Smiles

Teaches

Cooks

Shops

Drives

Calls

FACILITATING SUBJECT + VERB + OBJECT (SELF)

When you want to let others know you are doing something, begin by stating "I," followed by your action word and the item. For example, if you want to say you're eating an apple, you can say "I" (point to the child), "eat", and "apple". This is how you can explain what you're doing.

Let's draw or add a photo of you here, and we'll practice saying examples of what you're doing.

Play

Piano

Drink

Juice

Eat

Pancake

Draw

House

FACILITATING SUBJECT + VERB + OBJECT (SELF)

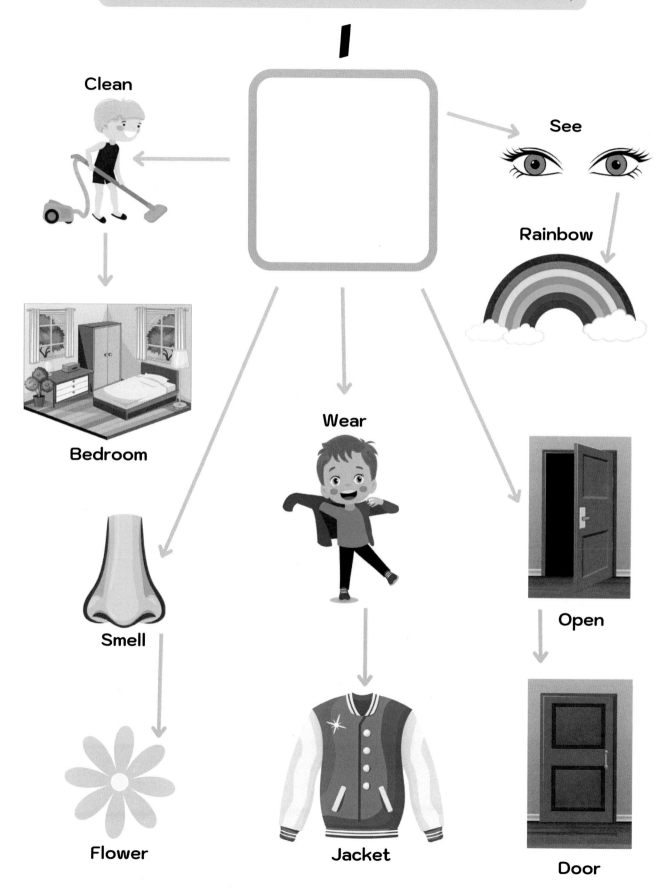

Clean

See

Rainbow

Bedroom

Smell

Wear

Open

Flower

Jacket

Door

FACILITATING SUBJECT + VERB + OBJECT (OTHERS)

When you want to say somebody else is doing something, you can say their name, the action they are doing, and then the item. For example, if you want to say Mom is washing her hands, you can say "Mom", "wash", "hands". I will point and we will say it together, then it will be your turn to do it on your own

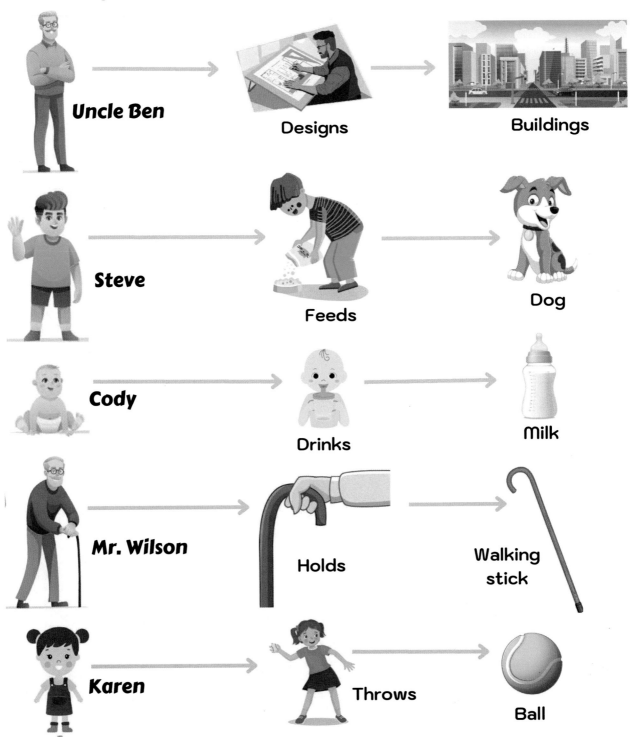

Uncle Ben   Designs   Buildings

Steve   Feeds   Dog

Cody   Drinks   Milk

Mr. Wilson   Holds   Walking stick

Karen   Throws   Ball

FACILITATING SUBJECT + VERB + OBJECT (OTHERS)

John — Plays — Guitar

Stella — Gives — Medicine

Mr. Taylor — Flies — Airplane

Dr. Thomas — Fixes — Teeth

Harry — Delivers — Pizza

FACILITATING SUBJECT + VERB + OBJECT (PLACES)

There are times when you want to say that you or someone else is going somewhere. When stating that you want to go to the park, you can say "I", "go", "park." You can also say that someone else is going to the park by mentioning their name: "Dad," "go," "park." Let's practice together.

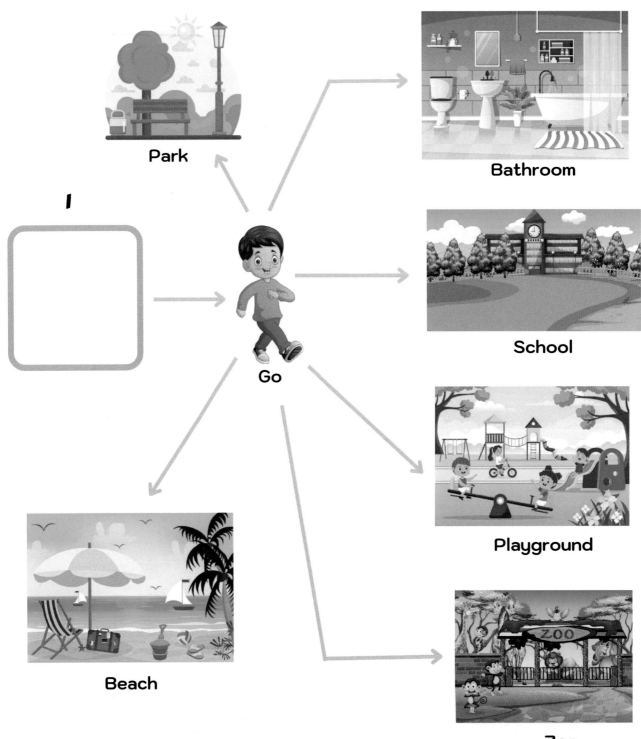

I

Park

Bathroom

Go

School

Playground

Beach

Zoo

FACILITATING SUBJECT + VERB + OBJECT (PLACES)

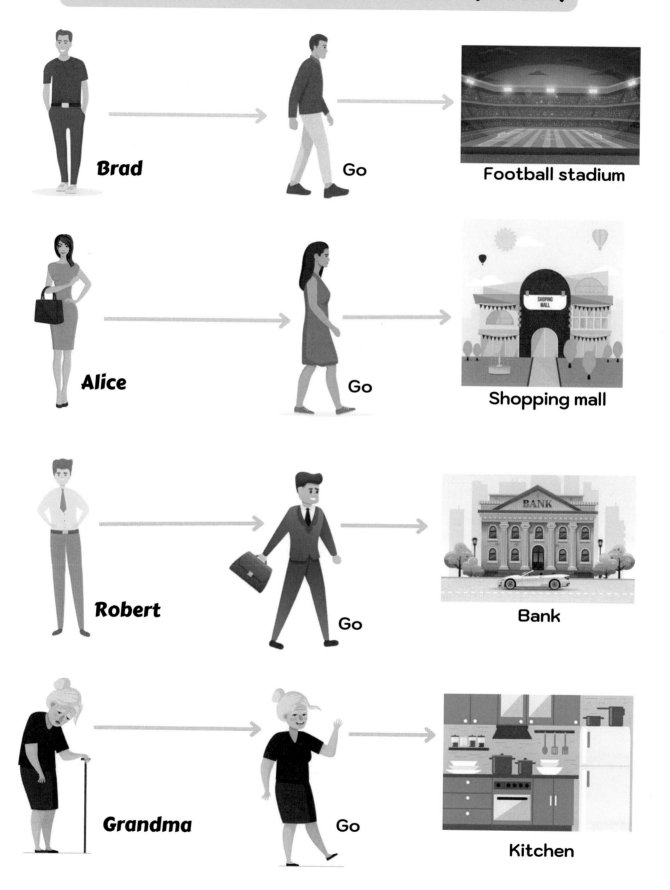

Brad — Go — Football stadium

Alice — Go — Shopping mall

Robert — Go — Bank

Grandma — Go — Kitchen

Thank You!
Found this book helpful? Don't forget
to give us a 5-Star Review. It helps us
create more useful workbooks like these.
It also helps our small business thrive.
We appreciate it so much!